REMEMBER!

An Encounter with Jesus Christ

BERT CARSON

Janie,
You are a
light that never
flickers!
Love
Bert

Many people worked to make this book possible. Chief among them were my wife, Edwene Gaines, without whose editorial assistance it would not have happened. More important than her editorial assist was her unfailing support. That support along with the enthusiasm and cheers of John & Jan Price and Karl and Terry Kandell were instrumental in placing the message in your hands. Special thanks to Maureen Dempsey for the cover design. Thanks Mo—you are great!

Bert Carson

You have heard the call of our teacher, "Follow Me," and you have accepted the invitation. This book is dedicated to you.

CHAPTER 1
August 15, 1968

Thirteen-year-old James Howard, Jr., Jamie to friends and family, sat on the back porch steps with his face held in his hands and his elbow resting on his knees. He was the picture of boredom as he gazed blankly toward the woods that adjoined his back yard.

There were a number of reasons for his discontent. The mid-August heat was hanging over south Alabama like a wet blanket and there wasn't a cloud in the sky or even a hint of a breeze to promise relief. He had read all the books in the library that he was interested in reading. But worst of all, his best friend, Georgie had left last Saturday for a one week camp and wouldn't be back until next Saturday and today was only Monday. Then, to really cap things off, school started in two weeks.

Daddy always said there was some good in everything, he thought. So I wonder what's good about this heat. The dogs are too hot to chase bicycles for one thing. So what, it's too hot to ride a bicycle.

What's so good about Georgie being gone all week he wondered. Then the thought that had been floating just out of reach all morning came to the surface. Last night he had joined the church. The First Baptist Church of Sykesville. The church he had attended all

1

his life. Not because he wanted to attend but because Mamma and Daddy made him go...and go...and go. Twice on Sunday and every Wednesday night and it seemed almost like every other day too.

Then last night something happened. After sitting through years and years of invitations, altar calls, threats and accusations, last night on the last verse of the invitation hymn, "Almost Persuaded," he had suddenly realized that he was walking down the aisle. Stumbling really, because he was crying so hard he could barely see. The preacher was waiting down front. It seemed like it took forever to get there.

And now in the light of day he remembered something else about that walk. He remembered what the little voice said as he stepped out to walk. The little voice that was always there to give advice and comment. The little voice that he was always aware of but seldom listened to...the little voice had said, "You don't have to do this, you will be better off not to."

The voice was drowned out by the preacher asking, almost shouting, "Jamie, are you sure you are saved? Did you feel the Holy Spirit come into your heart? Isn't it wonderful to be a born-again Christian?" Jamie's eyes were filled with tears and he was so choked with emotion that he could only nod yes to the preacher's questions.

When the questions finally ended, the preacher straightened and faced the congregation. Then in his

2

best bass voice he said, "Thank God for this saved soul. Thank God for snatching this child from the door of hell and placing him eternally in the salvation promised by our Lord and Savior Jesus Christ. Now before you leave, come down front and shake young Jamie's hand and welcome him into the body of born-again believers."

They came to shake his hand and hug his trembling body. It seemed like there were a million of them. He began to cry again. That was last night yet the scene was still branded in his mind. His daddy standing on one side looking proud. His mother standing on the other side crying. And all the people shaking his hand and hugging him.

It was obvious Mama and Daddy were proud of him and very happy with his decision, but deep inside he knew, nothing had really happened even though he had cried and told the preacher he had been saved. And even though the voice was quiet now he could still hear, "You don't have to do this..."

That's what's good about Georgie being in camp, he thought, I don't have to tell him about it...and I know he doesn't know anything about getting saved. Georgie's a Catholic but he never talks about getting saved. Maybe by the time he gets back everybody will have forgotten about it anyway.

With that final thought on the subject, and not being able to think of anything good about the approaching return of school, he slowly stood, surveyed the area, stepped off the stairs and began the short walk to the woods. In spite of the heat his ever present companion Peck, a four-year-old, "mostly collie", fell in step at his heels.

As Jamie climbed the fence between his yard and the woods his mother looked out the kitchen window. Seeing Jamie, she paused recalling the pride she felt when he was saved last night. Again she enjoyed the vision she had long held of Jamie preaching to thousands all over the world. Even better than Billy Graham, she dreamed. She shook her head slowly to clear the daydream just as Jamie and Peck disappeared into the woods.

CHAPTER 2

There were times when Jamie didn't like his Mother at all. This was one of those times. Georgie had gotten home from camp that afternoon. Jamie helped him unpack while Georgie told stories of the past week. Camp sounds great...even if it isn't a Baptist camp, Jamie thought.

Jamie didn't have a lot to tell. Just about the old bones that he and Peck found over in the woods. "Probably old cow bones; anyway they aren't worth looking at in this heat," he said. So with unpacking done and talking caught up with they wandered over to Jamie's for Kool Aid and cookies.

That's when his mother had done it. She hadn't even asked Georgie about camp or anything. As soon as they sat down at the table she said, "Georgie, I guess Jamie's already told you about getting saved last Sunday night, hasn't he?"

With a blank look on his face, because he didn't know what getting saved meant, and Jamie hadn't mentioned it, Georgie said, "No M'am, I don't reckon we talked about that yet."

For a second a look of disbelief flashed across her face, Then it was gone and she launched into the full explanation of Jamie's conversion experience, that included an explicit account of every step down the

5

aisle, every tear shed and every hand shaken. An explanation that ended with, "And now Jamie has been saved. All his sins are forgiven and he will go to heaven when he dies and there he will live forever with Jesus." As the boys slipped out the door the story ended with, "That's the only way to everlasting life. You must be saved."

The two boys walked slowly through the dust and heat of late afternoon. They climbed the fence and walked into the woods on their favorite path. It seemed to Jamie they had walked for hours before Georgie said anything. Finally he did speak and it was to ask the question Jamie most feared. "Jamie, what did your Mama mean about getting saved?" he asked.

Jamie had thought about little else for a week. Since last Sunday he had waited for a change. Waited to be "filled with the Holy Spirit," waited to see Jesus, waited to hear God. Waited for anything to show him that something had happened last Sunday night. Something besides just walking to the front of the church and shaking hands with the preacher and everybody else in the place.

Finally Thursday night he faced the fact that nothing had happened and nothing was going to happen. Then he was afraid. Really afraid. Afraid God would send him to hell for lying about being saved. Or even worse, afraid Jesus would tell the preacher and his Mama and Daddy that he really hadn't been saved.

6

Wow! That would be the end of everything!

Now Georgie wanted to know what being saved meant. Now he had to make a decision. Tell Georgie he really didn't know, since he had just pretended to be saved, or give him one of the stock answers he had been taught. Jamie took a deep breath and said, "Being saved is like being born again. You start all over with all your sins forgiven and when you die you go to heaven."

In the moment of silence that followed this stock explanation he heard again the little voice, "You don't have to do this..."

Georgie looked at him with a puzzled expression, then said, "Let's go and see those old bones you and Peck found. They might be the bones of pirates or train robbers or something."

CHAPTER 3

Just as Jamie had suspected, the bones were cow bones. There weren't many and they appeared to be very old. Not much to look at on a hot summer afternoon, but they both knew they weren't looking at old bones; they were avoiding further discussion about being saved.

Being saved. The thought kept him awake well into the early hours of Sunday morning. Kept him awake thinking about having to face all those people in church again. He knew they would still want to shake his hand and congratulate him on being born again and he was afraid that there was a sign he was supposed to know. Maybe a password or code that God gave to those who were saved at the time of their conversion. In any case, he knew he didn't know the sign. Now everyone would know he had lied about being saved.

And as he lay awake trembling with fear he could still hear the small voice saying, "You don't have to do this..."

He finally went to sleep silently crying to himself, I do have to do it! I don't want to go to hell and I know I will if I'm not saved.

His excuse when he woke was, I'll tell them I'm sick and they'll let me stay home. His Daddy walked into the bedroom. "Son, have I got a surprise for you," he said. "So many people have been saved in the last three weeks there's going to be a special baptism service this morning and you're included."

That's it, Jamie thought. That's got to be it. I'll be filled with the Holy Spirit and really saved when I'm baptised. I've been worried for nothing. Even the Bible says Jesus got the spirit when he was baptised. In fact, God even told everybody how good Jesus was when he came up from the water. Will God tell everyone how good I am when I come up, he wondered, as he jumped out of bed and began dressing for church.

It was one of the longest services Jamie could remember. It seemed to drag forever. Every moment he was more anxious to be baptised and really saved. Then he could tell Georgie something.

He was the last of nineteen people to be baptised. When it was his turn he knew he would do it right. The preacher would put his hand over his mouth, pinching his nostrils closed. Then he would be plunged under the water while the preacher said "and now my brother I baptise you in the name of the Father and the Son and the Holy Ghost."

I'm going to concentrate on keeping my feet on the bottom of the pool, he determined. Those people whose feet came up sure looked silly. And I'm going to listen for God to speak as soon as my head comes out from under the water.

Sometimes the best laid plans go astray. This was one of those times. Not only did my feet come up, I got strangled and coughed; God didn't speak or send any sign and on top of looking dumb in front of everyone, I don't feel any different, he thought, as the preacher turned him toward the stairs and released him. He cried as he climbed out of the baptismal pool. The tears and the water streamed together down his face. His silent sobs almost drowned out the little voice, which was saying, "You don't have to do this. This isn't the way."

The voice did get through. It always did, whether he listened or not. His response to the voice was, I do have to do this. I want to be saved. I want to know more about God. I want to know all there is to know about God. . . and this is the only way I know to do it. At the top of the steps he sat down and wept. If his tears attracted any attention they were quickly and ignorantly dismissed as "tears of joy."

CHAPTER 4
August 15, 1971

God, I know this might make you mad, but then if you are as smart as everybody says, you already know. So if you want to kill me for it, you just go ahead and do it. You see God, sometimes I don't think you even care. I don't think you care what I do or what happens to me. God, I'm sixteen years old and it seems like I have spent all my life thinking about you, praying to you or just studying in your house. That's a long time to be close to somebody and never hear anything from them. Heck, Lord, I don't want a sign. I heard the preacher say it's a sin to ask for a sign. Lord, I just want you to talk to me. I know you're there Lord...I'm just not sure you care.

Jamie waited for what seemed like the ten-thousandth time to hear an answer to his prayer. Again, like all the other times he heard nothing. With a barely audible sigh that didn't come close to expressing all the frustration and emptiness he felt, Jamie gathered his long legs under his gangly frame and rose from the steps.

Before he turned toward the back door he gazed at the woods. Those few acres of woods were filled with so many memories they almost seemed to talk. But the one scene of all the scenes he had been a part of in those woods kept coming to mind more and more often these days. That scene was Georgie asking, "What does it mean to be saved?" I gave him an answer but it was a lie, Jamie thought, and now, three years later I'm no nearer the truth than I was then. And I have searched. I have walked down the aisle over and over to rededicate my life, to give my life to full Christian service, to be a preacher and to even be a missionary. I'll bet people are tired of seeing me down front, but that's when I feel the closest to God.

The trouble is it doesn't last, he thought, as he went in the house for supper.

Jamie considered his Daddy to be the finest Christian he had ever known, and he knew his Daddy had a close relationship with God. Finally he went to him to discuss his fears and ask his questions. "Daddy, I want to talk to you about God," he began. His Dad looked up from his evening paper and said, "O.K. son, what's on your mind?"

Jamie had to take a deep breath before he could continue. He was so choked up he was afraid he was going to cry. Finally he blurted. . ."Daddy, I'm afraid I'm not saved." That was all he could say. After all these years it was finally out and he cried.

His Dad put an arm around him, almost self consciously, and held him until the sobs eased and sniffles replaced tears. Then he said, "Son, you were saved when you walked down the aisle three years ago. You

14

know that once you are saved you are always saved. What you are going through now is one of Satan's temptations. You see, Son, if Satan can make you doubt your salvation, the next step will be to get you away from the church and into sinful living. That's the way the devil works, Son, and you have to always be on guard."

Jamie paused for a moment considering whether to pursue it further. Then he knew he had to. He had carried this too long to quit without the answer. With a deep breath, he said, "That's the other thing, Daddy, not only am I afraid I'm not saved, I don't understand why God would create us in his image and then send Satan to try to take us away from him."

As soon as he finished, Jamie looked down at the floor, afraid to meet his Father's eyes. There was a long silence. So long Jamie was afraid he hadn't been heard. He lifted his eyes from the floor and looked directly in his Dad's eyes.

In that moment he knew he had asked a question his Dad wanted an answer for, too. A question his Dad had no answer for... that was confirmed when he heard him say, "Jamie, there are some things we won't know until we go to be with God. I'm afraid that's one of them"

CHAPTER 5
August 15, 1985

It's ironic, Jamie thought. Fourteen years ago I realized that what I knew about God wasn't all true. I saw it in Daddy's eyes that night. There is one other question I wish I had asked him when I had the chance. It might have made the difference...but I didn't ask and now, I guess, I'll never know how Daddy could love being a Christian when there were so many things he didn't know or couldn't accept. If I had asked that question and gotten a good answer I could have saved myself a lot of pain and I could have saved a few of the people who loved me some sleepless nights.

The night sixteen-year-old Jamie asked his Father about salvation and Satan and realized his Daddy didn't know had marked the end of Jamie's search for a relationship with God. Jamie knew God was there, but he also knew that if his Daddy couldn't reach him, there was no point in his trying.

Jamie didn't turn his back on God that night, however he did end his quest for a conversation and a relationship with God. When he married, at twenty, he stopped attending church and for a long time seldom thought of God. A long time that included infidelity and despair. A long time that included prosperity and bankruptcy. A long time that included a few laughs

17

and a lot of tears. A long time that included five years of what seemed to be many lifetimes.

Now he was ready to end his life. At thirty he had chased happiness for the last time. He had known tears and sorrow for the last time. He wouldn't be disappointed again. God, you wouldn't give me any assurance or encouragement and I don't care anymore. I know you're out there, and tonight I'm going to be with you, whether you like it or not. When I get back in that car, God, I'm going to drive off the side of this mountain. They'll never be able to prove it wasn't an accident, so the kids will get the insurance money. I guess somebody might wonder what I was doing so far away from home. So what, I wonder about that, too. I guess it'll just go down as one more unanswered question in the life of Jamie Howard. Why did he die in a car wreck eight hundred miles from home, on a mountain he had visited only once in his life, twenty years before, with his family and his best friend, Georgie?

Georgie, he thought if you could only see me now. I don't know where you are. . .but here I am. . .on top of the mountain we loved so much as ten-year-olds. In fact, Georgie, I'm sitting on the edge of the dam with my feet in the water where we swam. He relived that moment from twenty years ago. He smiled, I almost drowned here. I would have if Daddy hadn't saved me. Now I've come back to die and this time there is

18

no one to save me. Do you remember, Georgie? I sure do. It seems like just yesterday and now it's almost all over.

Jamie closed his eyes and let his ears fill with the sounds of the mountain night...the water running over the dam and further down, the river plunging over the falls. The cicadas marked the heartbeat of the mountain with their insistent beat. He slowly opened his eyes. No sense in putting it off.

That and all other thoughts were put away as soon as his eyes opened. He gazed; then gasped. He rubbed his eyes. He gazed again and this time he almost fell off the dam and into the canyon at his back. About a hundred yards away in the middle of the lake was a man! A man walking on the water! Walking toward him!

Jamie was afraid! Terrified! Too terrified to move. He could only stare. As the man came closer some of the fear began to go away, replaced by the purest sense of peace he had ever known. As the fear left, Jamie began to notice some of the things that were happening. Even though the man was too far away to make out his features it was obvious that he was a tall man, both graceful and masculine. And he glowed! There was just no other word for it. The man was creating his own light, and he was radiant. Jamie thought about running then almost laughed when he realized, I came here to die anyway.

Now the man was less than fifty feet away. I have never seen a smile like that, Jamie thought. He must be an alien. That's it, he's an alien and he's going to take me away. O.K., I'll go.

Then Jamie noticed the man's feet. They were touching the surface of the lake. They were even making ripples, but he wasn't sinking or even having trouble keeping his balance. Then he noticed something else about the stranger's feet. Scars! Then he knew!

He knew and his heart felt as if it would burst with joy. Jamie raised his eyes from the scarred feet, up past the outstretched arms and looked into the most compassionate loving eyes he had ever seen...the eyes of Jesus Christ!

CHAPTER 6

Those eyes held Jamie in an embrace that was almost physical. He lost track of time and place. He felt stronger and more alive than he had at any time in his life. And for the first time in his life he knew what love was really all about. Love that transcended time and space. Love that overcame all fear...all fear! Love that filled him, assured him, and soothed him.

Time stood still and Jamie realized he was so caught in the love of Jesus that everything around him was blotted out. The sounds of the water, the wind, the cicadas...all gone. He was wrapped in love. Love had displaced fear. He couldn't believe it. No fear! None!

He wasn't afraid of this man. This man who walked on water. This man who glowed with an inner radiance. This man who was so filled with love that he had become pure love.

Then Jesus spoke and his voice was like none Jamie had heard before. Soft and compassionate, yet filled with power and authority. A voice that almost had a physical presence. "It's good that you aren't afraid. That means you are willing and open. I've come here tonight to make you an offer. An offer you shouldn't take lightly. However, if you accept the offer, it will mean you must continue your life on earth."

Jamie gasped. Without a pause Jesus said, "Yes, I know what you were planning to do tonight; and that's all right. It's not necessary though and I think you will change your mind after I explain my offer to you. Are you willing to listen, Jamie?"

Before answering Jamie thought, not only does he know I planned to kill myself, he knows I'm not afraid of him. He is in touch with my every thought.

Jesus smiled and spoke to Jamie's thoughts, "Why does it surprise you that I know your plans, your feelings and your thoughts? Don't let these things surprise you. They are nothing compared to what you will see and what you will do. Now, you haven't answered my question; are you willing to listen to my offer?"

With no hesitation this time, Jamie said, "Yes, yes, I've got nothing to lose and everything to gain."

"Don't be too hasty," Jesus replied. "If you accept the offer, you can't end your physical life tonight. You will be taking on a great work. A work that will consume you, for our Father's sake. A work that you will love, but one that will demand your all, your everything. Jamie, it's the work you came here to do. . .still it's up to you."

Jamie shook his head in puzzlement. Jesus responded to the gesture by saying, "That's right, you know your purpose here; you know all the secrets of the universe; you know everything that I and every

22

Master who has ever walked the earth know, but you have chosen to forget those things. That's what I will do for you now, Jamie, if you are willing, I WILL CAUSE YOU TO REMEMBER."

I Will Cause You To Remember.

CHAPTER 7

"I will cause you to remember!" The words rang in Jamie's ears. Then Jesus continued, "I will cause you to remember who you really are and what you are here to do. I will tell you what I really taught almost two thousand years ago and why I taught it. It's your decision, Jamie. If you like, I will cause you to remember all of that and more. I will give you back the power and authority you have chosen not to use. The power and authority you will need to complete your work."

For the first time in as long as he could remember Jamie did what the little voice inside told him to do. He did it without hesitation or reservation. "I accept the offer, whatever it is; I want to know why I'm here; cause me to remember!"

Without seeming to move, Jesus was suddenly sitting on the dam beside Jamie. His eyes were locked into Jamie's eyes with love and compassion. His words seemed to go straight into Jamie's brain without traveling through his ears. The concentrated attention between the two men was so great that all else ceased to exist. When he looked back on it, Jamie wasn't sure that Jesus always used words to express himself. It seemed that a large part of their communication was done in thoughts, thoughts that passed between them without words.

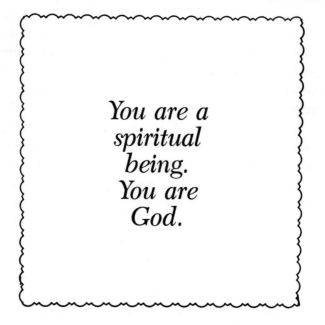

*You are a
spiritual
being.
You are
God.*

CHAPTER 8

"Jamie, the things you will learn tonight you will never forget. You will remember them all and you will share them with the world. Don't be concerned with how you will remember or how you will be able to tell the world. Just know that you will. You have a built-in guide, Jamie. That little voice that you have ignored so long that you finally listened to tonight. That is no trick of your imagination, Jamie. That is your contact with our Father. That is your intuition. Your intuition is infallible, Jamie, and like your arms or your legs or any other part of you, the more you use it the stronger it will be and the more you will trust it."

"Jamie, you were created in the image and likeness of God. That doesn't mean that God has a physical body like yours, or like the one you see me using tonight. That means that you are a spiritual being, Jamie, just as God is a spiritual being. I taught that in my ministry and now you just remind everyone again. Your body is a physical form of expression of your spirit. It isn't you. It's no more you than your words are you. Neither is it any less than your words. It's equal to and like your words; a form of expression. That's all your body is, that's all it was ever meant to be. Take care of it as you care for your words and

27

thoughts but remember, you are a spiritual being not a physical being."

"The spirit inside you is you. That's the part of you that was created in the image and likeness of our Father. The spirit inside you is our Father. The same spirit is in me. The same spirit, Jamie. Not a spirit like God. Not even a scaled down version. The spirit in you and me and every other person on the planet is God. Do you understand that, Jamie?"

"I think so," Jamie answered slowly, "What I don't understand is why I make so many mistakes and sin so much." "There are no mistakes, Jamie," Jesus replied. "One of my key teachings is do not judge. There is no right or wrong. The judgement of men makes that determination. Never judge."

"That's easy to say," Jamie responded, "but not so easy to do."

"Know this, Jamie, and it will be easy," Jesus answered. "No matter what anyone does, he acted only because he knew he was either right or proper or justified when he acted. There are no exceptions. That is truth and when you live that truth there is no need to judge. Jamie, recognize sin for what it really is; sin is acting out of physical consciousness or forgetting who we really are and acting like men."

Jamie looked puzzled. "I think I understand," he said. "I feel like I am beginning to remember something. Something from way back, back before I was

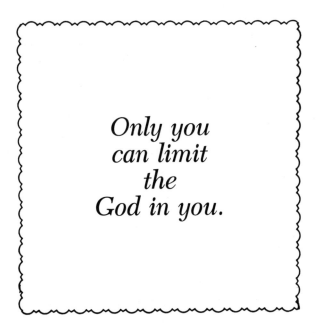

*Only you
can limit
the
God in you.*

even born."

Jesus smiled, and said, "You are remembering, Jamie. Remembering who you really are. Sin is forgetting. Forgetting who we are...thinking we are somehow separated from our Father. Alone. Sin is one of many ideas man has come up with to limit himself to his physical life. I taught that men were spiritual and some understood it. Now you must remind them. You are limited to the physical world only if you want to be."

"The spiritual part of each of us is God and God has no limits. The part of you that is the real of you is God. The part of you that never changes, that knows no limits, that can do anything, that is forever, that part of you is God. ONLY YOU CAN LIMIT THE GOD IN YOU. That is your decision. Your free will. You have the capability to limit God by denying his presence or by making him an outside power rather than the ever present essence of us that he is."

"Remember though, you can also remove those limits. The only difference in what I do and what you do are the limits you have placed on yourself, your real self; your God-Self."

"When you remember who you really are you can remove those limits. Jamie, you, like me, and every other person on the planet, are God. There is only one God in the whole universe. God our father who created everything."

"There is only one power in the whole universe, Jamie. That power is God, our Father. He is everything, Jamie. He is you, he is me, he is all there is. Without our Father there is nothing. Our Father has given us the world. Some of us understand that, more of us have decided to forget and limit ourselves to the physical plane. That's all right. We can do that, but as you have known since the beginning, we don't have to. Do you remember the parable I told of the rich man who gave talents to each of his three servants?"

Jamie nodded yes, and Jesus continued, "The servants who invested the money and multiplied it were no different than the one who buried his, except they had removed their limits. Our Father has given us everything we need to do anything we would like to do, and then he gave us the freedom to do or not to do. The freedom to be God or to be man. When we elect to be a man we build limits, then recognize them. To be God all we need do is remove our limits. Let me give you an example. At no time did I teach that a man must die to have everlasting life. Think about that, Jamie. You don't have to physically die. You don't have to take off the physical body. I physically died and picked my body back up to prove it yet somehow my teaching was misunderstood, limited if you will. In any case, touch my arm."

Jamie reached out and touched Jesus' left forearm. "See, Jamie, that is just as real as your arm and it's

31

two thousand years old. There is no reason to die. There never has been. There never will be. Death is only another limitation that people have chosen to buy into."

"So, Jamie, the first principle, and the basis for all others is this, you are God. You can live with or without limitations. You can buy into any belief system you want. You can deny your spirituality. None of that matters or changes the real truth of you. You are God! You always have been and you always will be, from everlasting to everlasting."

CHAPTER 9

"I am God. From everlasting to everlasting," Jamie
said softly, and then whispered, "I am getting it . . . or
should I say I am remembering. That's right, I am
remembering all of it. Who I am, who I really am."
Then he looked quickly at Jesus and blurted, "but
they won't believe me. I'm a failure. I've never done
anything great. They won't listen to me. But
you . . . you're the, the, the Son of God. Why don't you
tell them?"

There was a long pause. Then Jesus smiled. The
most beautiful loving smile Jamie had ever seen. Then
he said, "That's why, Jamie. That's exactly why I
won't tell them. They won't hear it from me. Now
you remember that you are a spiritual being. That
you, too, are the Son of God. That you and I are the
same. If you see any difference in you and me, you are
missing the lesson. There is no difference. They have
set me up as God. I never said that. Yet men believe I
said it. They heard me say it in their mind and they
have built a belief system around what they think they
heard."

"Their belief system makes me the only God. I said
that I and the Father are one. I also said all men are
one with the Father. I never said men are separated
from our Father by anything other than their self-

33

imposed limitations. If I came to the world as I have come to you tonight the world would know me no better now than it did before. Even worse, they would believe I came to be a king, not a teacher, just as they believed almost two thousand years ago."

"Jamie, a belief system is necessary to grow. It's the same thing to a man that a splint is to a broken bone. When the bone is healed the splint should be removed and cast away. A belief system must be treated the same. Until ultimately a man has no belief system at all. That is, he knows and understands that he is God. God has no belief system. God has no denomination. God has no country or politics."

"If I appeared to the world now I would only reinforce their belief system, not show them a way to grow beyond it. Men need to be reminded of who they are, not reinforced in their false beliefs of who they aren't."

"All men already have everything they need. Everything they need to express their true self, their God self. They only need to recognize that, release their limitations and grow beyond their belief system. You can remind them of that and start them moving upward again."

"When I came to the planet before, the people were looking for a king. They thought I would be their king so they never accepted me as a teacher. The irony of it is that a lot of religions, denominations and churches recognize that the people of my day expected a king and didn't recognize me as a teacher and they condemn them for their belief. Yet those same people have set up the same scene for me again. They expect me to come as king. They have built their belief system around it and my appearance now would only strengthen that illusion."

"Illusion? I don't understand. You said you would come again. I've always been taught that you would come again. Could you tell me what you meant?" Jamie asked.

Again Jesus smiled, then answered, "I said I would come again and take you unto myself."

"That's what I'm talking about," Jamie said. "Then what happened?," Jesus asked.

"Well," Jamie thought for a moment, then said, "You were crucified, you died, and three days later you arose." Jesus looked at him in love and waited. Jamie's eyes suddenly lit up, "You did! You did! You came again! And we missed it." "Not everyone missed it, Jamie," Jesus said. "Most of them did though because it didn't fit their particular belief system. And that belief system has been handed down from generation to generation. You can do something about that. Do you see now what would happen if I suddenly appeared to the world?"

"Yes, I do and I will do whatever you ask," Jamie answered. "I know that there is more and I need to know it. Will you remind me?"

Jesus responded instantly, "Jamie, before I leave you this night, you will know everything there is to know."

CHAPTER 10

"You are a spiritual being. You are God. That is the foundation for living. The cornerstone to go on that foundation is this, there is only one power in the universe and that power is God. There is only one truth, one love, one good in the universe. They are the same; God."

"You see, Jamie, in order to support the belief that he was physical and not spiritual, man had to build his belief system on the idea of two powers. That is, a power for good, which was God, and power for evil and he called that by many names. Satan seems to be one of the most popular. Now you can see why man had to create Satan. Without Satan man would be God and his belief system denied that. With Satan to oppose God, man was just an innocent pawn caught up in a universal game over which he had no control."

"Remember this, Jamie, no matter what belief system a man has adopted. No matter how much logic or time has gone into justifying that belief system, it does not alter the truth one iota and the truth is there is only one power in the universe and that power is God."

"When I taught I used the words satan and devil to refer to the erroneous thoughts of man. Any thought that separates man from God is erroneous. To think that our Father, our God, our creator would create a being of power to torment, test and destroy us is ridiculous. Why would God destroy himself? The answer, of course, is he wouldn't. Not ever. He would see us destroy our wrong thinking. He would see us destroy our belief systems. He would see us destroy our limitations and remove the blocks we have erected to keep us from knowing who we really are. When you understand what the words satan and devil and demon really mean, then you can read the Bible and understand the teaching. Then with your new understanding examine and reevaluate your belief system."

"Wow," Jamie exclaimed. "I really am remembering. You and I are the same. We are brothers." Then he looked puzzled for a moment, and asked, "But why do you know so much more than me? And why can you do so much more than me?" Jesus looked deep into Jamie's eyes. It felt as though he had actually entered his soul, and it felt good.

"I don't know any more than you do, Jamie. I just remember more than you at this point in our growth. Maybe I have had more lifetimes to remember in . . . it doesn't matter. We are the same, Jamie."

"We are God expressing through physical bodies. That's all. And why can I do more than you? Because I have removed my limitations. I have removed my blocks. I did that by recognizing who I am and what I can do. I can do nothing of myself, of this physical presence that you see here. But of our Father... our Father, Jamie. I can do anything. You can do anything. We all can do anything. Remember that, Jamie, we can each do anything, through God, our Father."

CHAPTER 11

Then Jesus said, "Jamie, you remember that you are a spiritual being; you remember there is only one power—that power is God and you are God. You are power, you are love, you are truth."

"But I'm only a man," Jamie said.

Gently Jesus replied, "If that's what you want Jamie..but we know that isn't true."

"What do you mean?" Jamie asked, and knew the answer even as Jesus answered.

"You came here tonight with a plan to end your physical life. You know that a physical existence is not enough. You had forgotten your real self...Now I have caused you to remember."

Afraid that Jesus was about to leave, Jamie quickly said, "Before you go, explain more about belief systems."

"A belief system is a guide, a measure and a tool for spiritual progress. Every man has a belief system. Everything he sees and does is evaluated and judged through that belief system. Belief systems are not truth. They are a way to truth. They are not absolute but they are a way to the absolute. No matter what belief system a person adopts it is never completely positive."

Jamie looked puzzled, and asked, "What about

41

people who believe in doing good for others, like preachers and missionaries?"

"Jamie, a person's belief system evolves ever upward toward ultimate good, toward our Father. However, no matter how good the belief system is, none is better than the others. For a belief system to exist it must judge. For a belief system to be good it must recognize and give power to evil or sin. You see, Jamie, our Father is all good and all love. There is no belief system in God. You must explain to men that their belief systems, no matter how good or how righteous they appear they are nothing more than tools. Tools to understanding who they really are and why they are really here. That's why I didn't give a long list of things to do and not to do. There is no need. All we need to do is recognize that we are spirit, that we are God, and make ourselves a channel for the love and power of God to manifest through."

"That is all of it, Jamie. There is no complicated formula. There is no creed. Above all, there is no belief system. There is only God. On this plane God is expressing through man. How we manifest that expression is up to us...what we do with God determines what God does with us."

CHAPTER 12

Jamie was silent for a long moment after Jesus had spoken, then said, "You have caused me to remember. I can feel God filling my whole being. I know some of that is because you are here beside me and you know who I really am, but I know that most of the change is because I am now aware of who I am. I know that it's a lasting change. I know that from here my only direction is up, but,"... he paused again. Jesus waited patiently for him to continue, finally he did. "In just a few minutes you reminded me who I was. In just a few minutes I have been born again. Since it's that easy, why didn't everyone get it from you before?" Jamie asked.

Jesus answered immediately. Looking back on it later Jamie realized that he must have been expecting the question. "Jamie, no one can 'get it' until they are ready to get it. No matter how great the prophet or teacher, no matter how timely the message, a man 'gets it' or doesn't 'get it,' from within, not from without. It's the belief from within, not from without. It's the belief system again, Jamie. When we make a belief system infallible we protect it rather than examine and change it. There will never be a time when everyone is at the same level of expression. Everyone sees from his own perspective and through his own

The key is this: Express God!

belief system. However, when enough of us grow we naturally take everyone else with us."

"The key is this, Jamie. Express God. Express the Father every minute of every day. To do that, turn loose of self, turn loose of Jamie. Don't be concerned for anything except your expression of God. It's like learning a new skill. The more you work at it the better you will become. The more you put yourself aside the more of the Father will come through. The more you adapt your belief system to expressing God the less you will need your belief system. When your belief system is gone, you are done here, Jamie. Then you can go on or stay and teach. Because then all your earth lessons will have been learned."

"Start at the beginning and stay there," Jesus said. Jamie looked puzzled again.

"Jamie, in the beginning was God. That's all Jamie, just God. That's all there is now Jamie. Everything else is man looking for God. Man going back to the beginning. There is no evil, there is no death, there is no lack, there is only God. Man created all the rest, and anything that man creates is not real. That is, it's not permanent. Only God never changes. Only God is real. You can express as much or as little of the reality of God as you choose. Remember, Jamie, the choice is yours but sooner or later, in this life or another, you will learn the lesson and express all God.

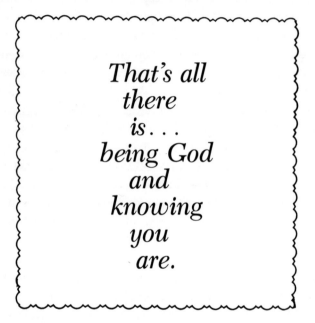

*That's all
there
is . . .
being God
and
knowing
you
are.*

CHAPTER 13

"This life or some other," Jamie repeated. "Do you mean there is more than one life for us; there is such a thing as reincarnation?"

Jesus smiled, "You have been talking to me and you ask that question?" Then he smiled, "Of course there is reincarnation as we call it. A better way to think of it is this. The part of you that is God. The part that we sometime call soul, the spirit of us, if you will, never dies. Men through the ages have elected to kill their physical bodies. That's a choice that man may elect or not elect. It's his option. To kill God is not optional. God is forever. And the part of man that is God is forever and will express itself in as many bodies as necessary to learn all the earth lessons."

"You mean you lived before you were Jesus Christ?" Jamie asked in wonder.

"Of course, many many times. I said so in my ministry. Few understood then. More and more are understanding now. You, too, have lived many times on this earth, Jamie. It's not important what you did and who you were. You were expressing God just as you are now. You were growing and experiencing, and being. . .that's all there is Jamie. Being God and knowing you are. . ."

*Forgiveness
clears the
channel
between you
and
God.*

CHAPTER 14

There was a long pause. A pause in which both men were comfortable. Then Jesus said, "Jamie, there are many things I could tell you. Things that would fill your mind with wonder and amazement. However, it's more important that I speak to your heart because your mission is of the heart. To that I have three of the most critical and often overlooked earth lessons to share with you. These lessons will be a key to the success of your mission."

"The first lesson is the one that I shared so often in my earth ministry. Yet it has been almost completely overlooked or misunderstood. That lesson is FOR-GIVENESS. Jamie, it's vital that you understand the importance of forgiveness for your life so you may share it as you go into the world."

"Forgiveness clears the channel between you and God. To fail to forgive is to block the Father. Each of us must examine our lives carefully and forgive every-one who we feel has done us an injustice. To harbor these feelings is in direct opposition to spiritual law. Failure to forgive is the cause of sickness, death and poverty. Failure to forgive is another way of denying God."

"Denying God? I don't understand how failure to forgive is denying God," Jamie said.

"It's like this, Jamie. When you fail to forgive you are saying in effect, the person or event that you are not forgiving has control over your life. Failure to forgive is to recognize a power other than God." Now you know that you, and only you, are responsible for your life.

Jamie thought for a moment then smiled, "I've got it. And for years I have done just that. Boy, do I have a lot of forgiveness to do." Then he paused for a second, and added, "You know, it seems to me that I need to forgive myself as much or more than I need to forgive anyone else."

"Now you're getting it," Jesus replied. "Forgiveness always starts with you and it always ends with you. Forgiveness is not a one-time process either. It's something you practice every day. Just like directing your faith, which we will talk about in a moment, you work on forgiveness all the time. The more you work on forgiveness, the less you have to forgive. The reason for this is, the more you forgive and get rid of, the more spirit of God you become a channel for..."

"I've got it," Jamie said, "The more God there is in me the less room there is for resentment, jealousy, fear, hate...and all the other things that need forgiveness."

"That's it, Jamie, now you are ready for the second lesson of the heart."

CHAPTER 15

"The next lesson is one you have heard of for years. In fact, you have tried to practice it after a fashion," Jesus said.

"I can't imagine what it is," Jamie said.

"Well," Jesus replied, "it's a lesson that you sometimes call GOAL SETTING."

"Goal setting? I don't remember you ever talking about goal setting in the Bible," Jamie said.

Jesus smiled and answered with a question, "Do you remember me saying, Ask and you shall receive?"

"Sure I remember that," Jamie replied, "but what's that got to do with goal setting? Goals are nothing but things that we want to happen," Jamie said.

Jesus replied, "There are many different processes being presented as effective goal setting but I have already presented the most effective method. First, ask believing and you will receive. It is our Father's good pleasure to give you the kingdom. One of the main purposes of my ministry was to remind men that they had direct access to their Father and all they had to do was ask, believing, and it would be done.

"Now, many have determined that we should decide what we want and make a plan to get it. That isn't necessary. All we need to do is ask. More often than not we will receive our desire without so much as

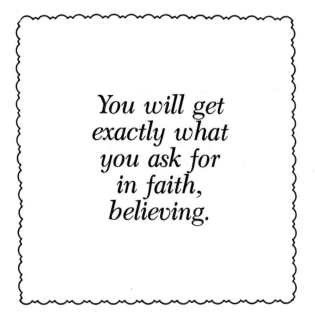

You will get
exactly what
you ask for
in faith,
believing.

a hint of a plan. After all, why ask for a plan when you really desire the goal? Your Father is the master builder, Jamie. You are the architect. Your Father is the builder. That is a principle that always works."

"There is nothing in your life that you did not ask for believing that you would receive it. Now you know that you have been the architect, you can clear up some of your past construction and begin the building the way you really want it to be. Remember this, Jamie, no matter how ambitious you think your goals are, they are nothing to God. He is only waiting for you to ask. He won't change your goals. He won't cut corners. He won't put your job out to the lowest bidder. You will get exactly what you ask for in faith, believing."

In silence, Jamie let Jesus' words sink in, then he said, "That makes so much sense. How did we miss it?"

Jesus quickly answered, "It was overlooked much like forgiveness. Men have become so blinded by their vision of this earth that they have forgotten the reality of their being. They have forgotten that they are the sons and daughters of God just as I am the son of God. And though I said it over and over men failed to see it because they refused to believe that they were worthy to be God."

"Now, Jamie, it's your turn to tell them. It's your turn to cause them to remember. It's your job to tell them. It's their job to remember. You can't make them. Only they can make that choice. That's what makes man unique in the universe...the ability to choose."

"Wait a minute, Jesus, you said you would give me three keys and that's only two," Jamie said.

"That's right," Jesus answered, "I saved the most critical lesson for last."

CHAPTER 16

"The key of keys is the simplest and most overlooked of all, Jamie. That is, LIVE IN THE PRESENT MOMENT. It sounds so simple that the significance of it has been almost totally hidden from man, except in the most superficial way."

"Time exists only in the earthly dimension. However, until you can transcend time and space, which is another lesson, you should understand the principles of time."

"God has no limits, Jamie. That includes the human limit of time and space. The ability to transcend time and space comes with the ability to transform the earthly body to the spiritual body."

"Do you mean to die?" Jamie asked.

"Not at all," Jesus replied, "Death as you call it is the conscious release by the spirit of the physical body. The spirit then goes on and the physical body returns to the earth. The transformation I am talking about is the transformation of the physical body into a spiritual body, not the discarding of the physical body."

"Is that what you did when you were crucified?" Jamie asked.

Jesus answered, "Exactly and all men can do the same, Jamie. But, that isn't the lesson tonight. We will cover that one later."

"The lesson now is, until you transform your body or until you elect to discard it physically dying, your spirit is housed there. Your spirit can operate in any dimension and on any plane, yet because of the bond of spirit and body, you must operate on the physical plane."

Seeing the lack of understanding in Jamie's eyes, Jesus continued, "You cannot carry your physical body with you beyond the earth plane until you have learned to transform it as I have. You may send your spirit out of your body in dreams or self-induced soul travel but the spirit must return to the body because they are bonded together."

"That's why you must concentrate on living in the present moment. Your body keeps you in the present moment and it's essential that your spirit be totally with your body for maximum effectiveness. You will have to work at that every moment. It's a constant exercise but it gets easier. It's also necessary that you learn living in the present to learn transformation of the body. Living in the present moment is being who you really are...Do you see why it's the key of keys, Jamie?"

"It's almost overwhelming to think about...but I am beginning to see the importance of being in the present. It's so overwhelming I think that may be why men, or at least I avoid being in the moment," Jamie answered. Jesus smiled at him, the same smile his

*Stay in
the
moment,
every
moment!*

algebra teacher had used when it became obvious that he had finally made his point and been understood.

"As you work on living in the present you will be amazed at how little time you have been spending there. Don't worry. Like learning to walk, you will master the present moment. Also like walking, you will find that the more you work at it the better you become."

"For total mastery of the physical plane and for the knowledge you need to move beyond it, stay in the moment, every moment!" Jesus said.

CHAPTER 17

"Listen to God . . . to the voice inside you. Your intuition is infallible. The more you listen to and follow the instructions of our Father the more you will hear. Always stay in touch with God."

"That's it, Jamie," Jesus said softly . . . "Forgive always, yourself and everyone else who you think has offended you; focus your faith by asking the Father for all that you need or desire, and finally live fully in every moment."

"Now take those lessons, Jamie. Learn them, live them and teach them to others so as to cause them to remember. To remember who they really are . . . the children of God in whom God lives. They are God, Jamie, go remind them. Remind them that the only power in the universe is God."

"This is my promise to you, Jamie. When you have learned those lessons and taught them, I will meet you once again in this place. Then I will teach you transformation and together we will walk on this water."

With those words he stood and took both of Jamie's hands in his, looked deep in Jamie's eyes, smiled and said, "Have fun learning and teaching. I will see you here again, soon." Then he added, "If you need me, just call and I will be there with you."

With that he released Jamie's hands, stepped off the

dam onto the water and with scarcely a ripple began walking away. As the distance between him and Jamie increased, Jamie began hearing the cicadas and the waterfall and all the other night sounds. He quickly realized that as long as Jesus had been there he had not heard those sounds, or any other sound save the voice of Jesus. Wow, he thought, that must have been my first lesson in totally living in the moment.

Jesus was over a hundred feet away and fading from sight when Jamie glanced at his watch. He blinked and looked again. The luminous hands had not moved at all since the last time he had looked at them . . . only moments before Jesus had appeared. He jerked his head up and looked across the smooth surface of the river. The only movement he could see was the silent scurrying of clouds across the face of the moon.

CHAPTER 18

Wow! I don't believe it, it seems like we talked for hours yet literally no time at all has passed since I looked at my watch last. He quickly took the watch off and held it close to his face. In the light of the moon, he could see the second hand sweeping down through six and in perfect order beginning its ascent past seven then eight and nine. There was nothing wrong with the watch.

I must have dreamed it. Just as quickly he knew it had not been a dream. Even dreams take time, he thought, and beside if I had gone to sleep I would have fallen forward into the river or backward into the canyon. I must have gone crazy, or even worse, maybe I killed myself and this is what dying is all about. Then he looked to the right and down. Down to the spot where Jesus had been sitting and he saw something that hadn't been there before.

Where Jesus' left hand had rested on the dam there was a stain. Even in the bright light of the moon he couldn't tell what it was. He touched it cautiously with his forefinger. He jumped and almost fell into the river. It's wet and it's too thick to be water, he thought. Again he stuck his finger into the small puddle. This time he held his finger close to his eyes as he had his watch moments before...and he cried when

61

he saw a drop of blood...blood from the wounded hand of Jesus Christ.

Great sobs swept over him. He cried as he hadn't cried in years. Tears ran unnoticed down his face. Tears that washed and cleansed. His body was racked by sobs...sobs that strengthened and renewed him.

At last he rose from the dam and started to his car. Not to go and kill himself as he had planned, but to go and remind others as he had agreed. With the sound of the river and the wind in his ears, he again heard the words of Jesus..."When you need me, just call and I will be with you."

Jamie smiled, then laughed, as his steps quickened with purpose.

CHAPTER 19

Jamie was nervous. Terrified would be a lot closer to the truth. Even though he had answered the altar call many times vowing to devote his life to being a minister or a missionary, the truth was he was scared silly at the thought of speaking to a group of people. Now here he was on the platform at his church. A church he hadn't been in in years and he was going to preach. Quickly he corrected himself, I'm only going to talk. I'm just going to share the message Jesus gave me to share.

He glanced out at the people already seated and then to the rear of the auditorium where another dozen or so were coming in. It looks like there would be a hundred or so in the audience. That's a lot more than we used to have on Sunday night when I was attending regularly. Looking closer at the crowd, he realized there weren't many of the old-timers there. Out of all those people there were only a handful of familiar faces. The Jenkins, Jim and Doris, in their usual place, three rows from the front in the center. Then there were the Hendersons, Ken and Jo Ann. They never missed a Sunday service.

And there was his mother with her two friends, Evelyn and Frances. All widows now but still devoted to the church where they had spent so many hours with husbands, now long dead, and children who for one reason or another never shared church time with them anymore. He looked back at his mother and realized she was wearing the same look she wore at little league games and school plays when he played or performed, a look that said, "I would like to be proud of you, but the fear that you will embarrass me overcomes my pride."

Then he caught his wife's eye. What he saw there was even more shocking. The look was as clear as the headline of the Sunday paper. He and Susan had been through a lot together. So much that he could read her face. Even though he had never seen quite this expression he knew what it meant. "You have disappointed me one time too many. If this is another let down it will certainly be the last."

Thinking back over the years of their marriage he knew her attitude was more than justified. All the big dreams and schemes. All the moving and starting over. All of the acting without planning. All of it capped off by his phone call last night. She hadn't heard a word from him in over twenty-four hours prior to that call; then it had been another of many life-changing phone calls. A call from a beaten man. A man who was crying. A man who was obviously on the brink of totally losing all self control. A man who had said only, "It's me, Babe. I've been fired again. I've got to go and think about it. Try not to worry. I'll call you when I can." End of conversation. He had hung up before she could respond. Her only word in the entire conversation had been, "Hello."

From that conversation he had driven seven straight hours. Driven to a mountain where he planned to take his own life. Then Jesus appeared; literally walked in...he smiled at the memory. And everything had changed. One of the things that had always fascinated Jamie about Jesus' disciples was their willingness to leave everything and follow him. Now, he understood.

In that instant, sitting on the platform of the Bethel Church auditorium, he remembered Jesus' last words to him, "When you need me just call and I will be there."

Jamie closed his eyes and instantly his imagination carried him back to the mountain. Back to the moment when he saw by the moonlight the blood drip from his finger. He remembered driving away almost reluctantly. Stopping at the first phone booth and calling Susan. She was relieved to hear his voice, then he heard the apprehension creep in as she began to listen to his words.

"Look, Babe, I'm a long way from home but I'm headed that way. I won't make it in time for church in the morning but you tell Brother Jim that I have had a real spiritual experience and I would like to share it with the church at the evening service." She tried to interrupt but Jamie cut her off with, "There's too much to tell on the phone. Don't worry, I'm OK. Better than OK, I'm better than I have ever been. Tell Robin and Bobby that I love them and I'm on the way home."

She made one more attempt to establish order in the conversation. "Jamie, where are you? What's going on? I've been worried sick...," she blurted, but he cut her off again.

"I'll tell you everything when I get home, Babe. Don't worry. Just do what I asked... and Babe, I love you." Her response was to slowly hang up the phone. That didn't bother him. He knew she would come through. She always had and he knew she would now.

As he looked at the crowd he knew he had been right. Susan had come through. But he knew now it might be the last time she ever would. The look on his daughter Robin's face told him she shared her mother's feeling and a sidelong glance at Brother Jim convinced him that he had more apprehension than confidence. The only bright spot in the group seemed to be his son. Bobby was staring at him with rapt attention. You would have thought he was looking at a cross between Santa Claus and Mickey Mantle judging from the attention and hero worship he radiated as he stared at Jamie.

Jamie shuddered and thought, "I don't know which

66

is easiest to handle, their fear or their faith." He slowly closed his eyes and silently said, "Jesus, you said you would be here if I called, now I am calling. I am ready to share the message that you gave me and I'm afraid...Jesus, take away my fear and give me the courage to do what I agreed to do and give me the words to get the message through."

Then he heard the small voice. The voice he had ignored for so long. The voice that was always right. He heard, "Jamie, you are my son just as Jesus is my son. I will be with you. I am always with you. I have always been with you and I always will be. Give up your human need to control and give the task to me. Do it in faith, Jamie. Do it as Jesus did, through me and not of himself. You will have the courage and the words. You and I are one, Jamie. Don't worry about getting the message through to others. Your only job is to deliver the words. It is up to them to get it. You are as much of me as you are willing to be, Jamie. Be all of me."

Jamie softly murmured, "Thank you, Father, I release all my ego and trust you completely. Amen."

Later some people said he was transformed in that moment. Others said no. But Jamie knew, he knew when he gave control to God the fear went away. He was like a spectator watching a person perform flawlessly and the person was himself.

He heard the opening hymns and saw the collection

taken. He heard Brother Jim introducing him, "I'm not real sure what Jamie has to share with us tonight...," he said, then glanced nervously at Jamie before continuing in an unsure manner, "...but I know it will be interesting and...and...it's good to have you with us again, Jamie." Then with an apprehensive sigh, Brother Jim stepped away from the pulpit and turned toward Jamie while extending his hand.

CHAPTER 20

Sometime later when Jamie looked back on the "sermon", he realized that God had given him the words. Not only given the words but also the strength to speak them. It was almost as if he were in the audience watching himself perform. An unusual feeling but not uncomfortable, he reminisced.

Standing at the pulpit Jamie's eyes swept the audience very slowly. He waited so long before beginning that the congregation began to rustle with impatience and discomfort. At what seemed to be the last possible moment before the crowd would explode, he began.

Softly, yet clear and understandable even to those furthest from him, he spoke, "I know you are wondering what in the world I have to say to you. You haven't seen me here in years. You have probably heard rumors about me that convinced you that you would never see me here again, certainly not in the pulpit."

Glances were exchanged by those of the congregation who prided themselves on knowing what was happening in the lives of all the church members. Susan and his mother kept their eyes fixed resolutely straight ahead.

"I won't keep you in suspense any longer," he continued. "I have not had my mind on God, the church or anything remotely spiritual for a long time. It wasn't that I didn't believe. It's just that no matter how hard I tried I couldn't seem to make it work."

"Even in good times I couldn't seem to break through to God and when the bad times came it was even more hopeless. I guess that's why I quit coming to church. It seemed so hopeless. I wanted to know God personally but I never did, no matter what I tried."

"This weekend. Last Friday to be exact. I left town and headed for a place where I always go when things aren't going well. I knew I had to clear my mind because there was no way I could go on in the condition I was in."

He paused and gazed slowly over the faces in front of him, then continued, "I'll be honest with you because even though I don't know all of you I feel as if you are my family. I never figured I would be coming back."

There were a few audible sighs from the congregation.

"I didn't plan to run away. What I had in mind was committing suicide, killing myself and making it look like an accident."

At that the sighs, coughing and uncomfortable shifting became so distracting Jamie had to pause. Quickly two women seated near the back scurried for the rear exit. One had a five-year-old by the hand. As they neared the door the child stopped, turned back toward the pulpit, smiled and waved at Jamie with his free hand. Realizing what was going on, his mother snatched him through the door as Jamie returned his smile.

Continuing as though nothing had happened, Jamie said, "I didn't mean to shock you or upset you by telling that. I wanted you to know what mental and emotional state I was in when I left here. By knowing that, I'm sure you can better understand the magnitude of what happened to me. Obviously I didn't take my life. I trust that it's evident that my emotional state is rational and calm."

"Last night, I was sitting on a dam by a lake in the mountains a long way from here. I was planning how to end it all when I met a man." Jamie paused, reliving the moment when he first saw Jesus.

Quickly he snapped back, realizing the audience was waiting expectantly to hear the rest of the story. "A man who told me all the things I had been searching for... a man who knew my innermost thoughts, plans and secrets. A man who clearly loved me in spite of how I appeared to be..." Jamie paused again and seemed to look into every pair of eyes in the auditorium before continuing..."Last night I met Jesus Christ."

CHAPTER 21

Silence like a heavy fog fell over the auditorium. It seemed like minutes but in reality it was only a few seconds. Then as if on cue the room erupted. Everyone was on his feet talking and shouting. Not at Jamie but to each other. In fact, it seemed that not one of them would even look at Jamie, as if to do so would bring them to a horrible end.

Jamie tried to regain order. "Please, please, let me finish,...please let me finish...this is so important...so important." The last words were so soft no one heard as Jamie realized they weren't going to listen. He was shocked when he realized they were afraid, terrified would be closer to accurate. They had the same looks on their faces as disaster victims pictured in newspapers and magazines.

He turned to the rear of the platform and was surprised to see Brother Jim's chair was vacant. He turned slowly back to the auditorium and the first impression he got was of a scene from a movie he had seen years before. A scene of panic in a theater when fire erupted. Everyone had completely forgotten the show in the mindless flight for survival. He shook his head to shake the scene from his mind.

The congregation was almost fighting to see who would get out first. He recognized the Hendersons and the Jenkins leaving through the side door. He raised his head and focused his attention on those streaming through the rear exit. He moaned softly as he recognized Susan and Robin disappearing through the door.

Jamie closed his eyes blotting the scene from his mind. He grasped the edge of the pulpit and made a conscious effort to relax. As the sounds of the mass exit began to fade he prayed silent. "Jesus, I did what you said and I failed. I failed. They wouldn't even listen."

His body shook with a sob and tears ran from his tightly closed eyes. The hush deepened in the auditorium as the hasty retreat increased its distance. Jamie continued to pray silently. "Jesus, I know the message was your message because I felt your presence here with me. What went wrong? Why did they all leave?" He paused, bowing his head even further. Then he felt a calm secure feeling wash over his body and fill his mind. The same feeling he had experienced at the dam and he heard...

"You didn't fail Jamie. You did what you agreed to do. You brought the message to the people. Understanding and accepting the message was not your agreement nor your responsibility. It is no different for you than it was for me, Jamie. Receiving the message is not the responsibility of the teacher. Now Jamie, open your eyes and teach."

Jamie slowly opened his eyes. For a second he thought he was seeing things. There were still people in the auditorium. He couldn't believe it. The sudden charge for the exit had been so unexpected he was sure everyone had left. Yet he saw a young couple in the front row, a middle-aged man in the center and on the right side of the room near the windows, his son Bobby and his mother. Tears filled his eyes again and a lump blocked his throat.

Bobby stood, breaking the silence as he said, "Tell us what Jesus told you, Daddy."

Jamie stood motionless so long those left in the room began to think he had not heard the question. Had it not been for the tears slowly trickling down his cheeks, they could have easily assumed him to be unconscious. Finally, he raised his right hand to his face and wiped the tears away. Looking at each of the five people remaining in the room he began speaking. Softly and deliberately. His words seemed to seek out each of the ones left in the room and to envelope them.

CHAPTER 22

"Excuse me. I thought everyone had left. Thank you for staying and caring. As I was saying, last night I met Jesus Christ. I was sitting beside a lake in the mountains. Sitting on the edge of a small dam. I was all alone. As depressed as I have ever been in my life. My mind was made up that I was going to commit suicide. I could see no other way out. Just as I was ready to leave the dam and go and do what I had decided to do, I saw a figure, a man, walking on the water coming toward me."

"As he came closer I knew who it was. He was younger and more rugged than I had pictured him to be, but there was no doubt in my mind that it was Jesus Christ. His feet were touching the surface of the lake. Small ripples were formed by each step he took so I knew that he had a body just like mine."

"He came directly to me and told me what I was planning to do. He said it was all right if that was what I wanted to do, but if I was interested he had an idea that would cause me to change my mind about killing myself. So I listened. Before I tell you what he said, let me tell you how I felt. I have never known so much love in my life. Just sitting next to him without his saying a word, I became like a little baby who has just been fed and wrapped in a blanket and is being rocked to sleep. There was so much love coming from him that I could almost see it."

"Anyway, what he told me was this. He said that he came to earth to teach. In the years since he was here his message had become twisted, misunderstood, and misused. He told me he would tell me what to say if I would go and say it. My first reaction was to ask him, Why me? Almost as quickly as that thought came, I had another, Jesus, why don't you do it yourself?"

"To my first question he said, Why not you, Jamie? I couldn't answer that one. While I was thinking about it he answered the second one. Jamie, one of the main points you must deliver is this, I never came to be God. I came to teach and to show the way. The only difference between me and anyone else is that I know who I am and few have realized yet who they are; so they decided to set me up as God rather than to listen to and follow my teachings. If I return they will feel that I have come again to rule the world. Then the message will be missed again. So you see, Jamie, it's up to you to deliver the message. Will you do it? Of course I said 'yes' and that's why I'm here tonight."

"I thought everyone would listen and get it. I was really surprised when they all left. All but you that is," he quickly added.

"He said we are all spiritual beings in a physical body. The physical body is the earthly home of our

78

spirit, or soul, which is the real part of us. Our spirit is the part of us that was created in the image and likeness of God. The part of us that is God. He said that God is always in touch with us through what we have labeled our intuition. . . and it's never wrong. Whether we listen or act on what it says or not, it's never wrong. He said to talk to the Father all we have to do is talk to that still small voice within us — that is God — that is the real of us — that is the truth of us that is always there. . . always."

"He said sin is not a long list of things we can or cannot do. Sin is wrong thinking. Sin is thinking we are less than the children of God. It is thinking we are sick and poor. Sin is thinking we have to die. That's right, sin is thinking we have to die. He said he never taught that we have to die. He said he taught everlasting life — NOW — not after some physical death."

Jamie paused, reliving the time at the dam. Continuing slowly he said, "Jesus said it was so simple and so obvious there was no reason for anyone to miss the mark. He said no one was going to miss the mark either. If we don't learn in this lifetime, we get another and another and another until we do learn. . . learn who we really are. He said we all know. We have chosen to forget. So in reality, there is nothing to learn, only things to remember."

"He said the very first lesson in Genesis is the lesson of good and evil. The lesson of judgement. And it's repeated countless times throughout the Bible. It's the key to remembering who we are and why we are and most important where we are. There is no good, or evil." He paused for the sharp intake of breaths that came almost as one, then spoke again.

"The only thing that makes a matter good or evil is how you think about it. How you judge it. You judge everything as you were taught to judge, based on someone's idea of good or evil. For example, we used to heat and cook with whale blubber, so it was good to kill whales. Now it's bad. Not long ago it was bad for women to work. Now it's good. The judgement of men and their subsequent action has started wars, caused famine, enslaved nations but most of all, judgement has hidden the truth from man. There is no good. There is no evil. There is only God. Anything that isn't God is man's physical struggle to find God. In the story in Genesis, the result of the establishment of good and evil, or judgement, was death. That hasn't changed. As long as we operate on a system of judgement of good and evil we will die, we will kill, we will fight, we will hate...we will miss the mark of God. The mark of our real self. The starting point is to realize there is no good. There is no evil. There is only God and God is love."

"He said he taught that we should love our neighbors as we love ourselves. That we love ourselves by knowing who we are, by knowing that we are, right now, the perfect children of God. We learn love by knowing that everyone is the perfect child of God. Then he told me this about love. Jesus said, "Jamie, you must understand, truly understand, and know, that no one has ever done anything they didn't feel was either right or justified or necessary at the time they acted. When you know that you will know what love is. When you live that knowledge you will be love. You will see with a new vision the folly of a belief system based on something called good and evil."

"Jesus said the way to clarity about judgement was forgiveness. He said forgiveness was a key point in his teachings, yet it was one of the most overlooked and misunderstood. It's essential that we practice unconditional forgiveness to rid ourselves of judgements and clear the channel to our Father. We forgive everyone, including and especially ourselves, of everything we have classified as wrong, until we have no more so-called wrongs. Forgiveness paves the way to living without judgements. We stay on that way by doing away with ideals. Ideals are nothing but another form of judgement. We are children of God. God is perfect. We are perfect. That is no ideal. That is the total truth. When we operate in that truth there is no need for ideals or judgements. There is only love."

"He said we should direct our faith. Ask for what we want and we will receive it. Jesus said we are the

81

We are
perfect
expressions
of God.

rich children of a loving Father, a Father who will give us anything we ask for, but we must ask."

"Jesus said we have no limits. We can do everything he did and even more if we but remember who we are. . . we are God playing at being men. We are perfect expressions of God. However, until we remember who we really are we are stuck in who we think we are."

"Jesus told me that time is an invention of man. That with God there is no time. We are to live where there is no time." Seeing the puzzled looks Jamie hastily added, "The place where there is no time is now. In this moment, in this instant, there is no time, there is only now. It's only in this moment that we can be who we really are, the unlimited children of God. When we send our consciousness backward or forward, to or from this moment, then we are mortal, physical beings."

"That's what Jesus told me. He said he was our brother and our teacher. He came to show the way not to be the only son of God. He said it's simple. He said he told Thomas and it's recorded in the Bible. . . and where I go you know, and the way you know. He said it was easy; forgive, don't judge, love and see only love, ask for what you will and live where the Father always is, in the present moment."

Jamie stopped and stepped back from the pulpit. There was silence from the five. Then they stood as one, laughing and clapping. They began moving from their seats and coming toward him. Jamie felt the tears start again. Tears of happiness. They did get it, he thought. Just like I got it, they got it. He caught his son and his mother in a bear hug. They stood there crying and laughing together along with the young couple and the middle-aged man. They remembered together.

CHAPTER 23

In the weeks that followed, the story was the same. In churches, all but a few refused even to listen. However, he always shared with those few and they always got it. And though he had no way of knowing for sure, he felt they went and shared the truth of Jesus with everyone who would listen.

Jamie found many who would listen weren't in churches. In fact, they hadn't for the most part been in a church for years. He found them in parks and schools, he found them on their jobs and relaxing with their families. They were at ball parks and restaurants, libraries and bowling alleys. They were everywhere, waiting to hear, it seemed to Jamie.

Tonight they were in a North Georgia truckstop. He and Bobby were traveling back to the mountain where it had all started. About an hour away from the river they had stopped in a small truckstop. Though it was near midnight the place was crowded with truckers.

At the table next to theirs, two men became involved in a heated conversation that moved from who had the fastest truck, to who worked for the best company, to who lived in the best state. It was obvious there would soon be a fight unless a miracle happened. Then at the peak of their exchange, the men paused at the same moment to grab breaths. In that pause there was no sound in the restaurant no sound except the softly stated question, "Does it matter, does it really matter?"

They both turned to Jamie. "Of course it matters," the largest and loudest began...then his words trailed off as he said "...or does it?" There was another pause and the two truckers looked at each other and smiled, then laughed. With the pressure relieved, the normal noise of the truckstop returned.

Now a few minutes later there were at least fifteen truckers gathered around the table listening to the story of Jamie meeting Jesus. Listening and remembering. Remembering who they really were. Recognizing the truth about themselves.

Wake up . . .
We're here!

CHAPTER 24

Later as they drove toward the lake, Bobby asked, "Aren't you ever tempted to stay with a group when they remember who they really are?"

Jamie thought about the question a minute then said, "Yes, it is tempting. Then I remember two things. First, we are all children of God and there are many more people to remind; then I think of how twisted Jesus' teachings became in only the short time he was here...then the temptation to stay with a group goes away."

Bobby nodded knowingly and found a more comfortable position as the sounds of the highway and the wind lulled him to sleep.

In what seemed only minutes, Jamie was shaking him gently. "Wake up, Bobby, we're here." Bobby snapped up straight and gazed out through the windshield on what looked like a scene from a movie. He rubbed his eyes and looked again. The full moon was high in the winter sky casting moon shadows from the tall oaks. Shadows that didn't so much as quiver in the cold stillness of the night. The lake was so calm it was difficult to determine where the water started or stopped. For no obvious reason Jamie was whispering. "Come on, Son, we have an appointment to keep," he said. Without another word they opened their doors and began the short walk to the dam.

Though the temperature was in the twenties, neither of them was cold. They stood on the dam for a moment in the silence, then without a word they sat on the cold concrete surface. They didn't have long to wait. In moments a figure appeared on the water. A man walking on the water toward them. Jesus!

He paused some twenty yards away from them and stretched both arms toward them. With no hesitation Jamie and Bobby stood, stepped onto the water and walked to Jesus. The three embraced there in the middle of the lake. Then Jesus said, "You have done well. Now that you know who you are you can go on with me or you can go back to the task of reminding others who they are." Instantly they said together, "We will go back."

Jesus smiled and said, "I know. And I will always be with you." As they released their embrace, Jesus turned to the mountain side of the river, Jamie and Bobby back toward the dam.

Bobby turned back to Jesus and said, "Thank you. Thank you for caring enough to come back and show us the way."

Jesus answered softly, "It was my choice and my joy. Now go and remind our brothers and sisters."

Then said Jesus to them again, "Peace be unto you: as my Father hath sent me, even so send I you."

JOHN 20:21